AUTHOR'S NOTE:

I certainly hope you enjoy reading this play, but please be advised it is fully protected under Copyright. Anyone wishing to produce the show/perform it, in whole or in part, must obtain permission in writing.

All inquiries should be sent to

travelingwithghosts@gmail.com

DEDICATION:

To John Henry Holliday, who lived an extraordinary life we can only dream of.

To Della Lambert Jones, the Holliday historian who helped me keep the play accurate.

To Sally Davis, the light of my life.

TRAVELING WITH GHOSTS

Copyright 2007 James William Uht

The setting of the play is the Hotel Glenwood room for John Henry "Doc" Holliday. As the audience enters the theatre, there is a bed and nightstand center stage. The bed is made. There is a small table downstage right of the bed. Next to the table is a chair. On the table is a silver tray with a glass decanter full of whiskey and a small glass plus a shot glass. On the tray is a small cigar box, with small cigars, and a box of wooden matches. There is a coat rack next to the bed on the stage right side of the bed. On the coat rack is a long overcoat and hat. There is small bar setup downstage left.

When the audience is seated, the house lights and stage lights dim until total darkness is achieved. During the blackout Holliday enters and stands downstage center of the bed.

A few moments pass, then Holliday speaks from the darkness.

HOLLIDAY

On November 8, 1887 at approximately ten o'clock in the morning, John Henry "Doc" Holliday died of tuberculosis at the

Glenwood Springs Hotel in Colorado. He was thirty-six years old.

[The lights come up to full. Holliday is reading an 1800's era newspaper.]

This is funny.

[He looks around a bit and goes to the table. He puts the paper down 2and looks around some more.]

I never thought I would end up here. I never thought *where* I'd end up.

[Pours a drink and downs it. He then lights a cigar and pours another drink. Looks at the audience for a moment and then smiles.]

I have not properly introduced myself. I am John Henry Holliday. Most people know me as "Doc". You may call me anything you like. Many do. Oh, you cannot use any names that I have not heard before, on more than a number of occasions: dentist, gambler, drunkard, lunger, killer.

I was born on August 14, 1851 in Griffin, Georgia, the child of Alice and Henry Holliday. Contrary to popular notion, I was not born with a cleft palate. That vicious rumor was started by Mary Copperwaithe

Fulton Holliday, the wife of my cousin Robert. She was among the few Hollidays who would even mention my name and that was only to deny I ever existed. I was an embarrassment to her. I gambled. I drank. I consorted with "those types" of women. My exploits later in life so embarrassed her that she at first denied the stories. I was a member of the family "one does not talk about." Then I was not even a member of the family at all. When asked about me once, Mary replied, "That's not even his real name!" She denied even knowing me. Now that is the first truthful thing Mary said, for she and I never met. But she spoke at great length of my supposed birth defect and the surgery that supposedly was needed to correct it. She said it with such conviction you would have thought she was there from the moment of conception. Her story about my harelip was accepted as gospel by family members far and wide. No one ever questioned her.

I was baptized March 21, 1852 at the Griffin Presbyterian Church. My mother had been raised Methodist but joined the Presbyterian Church upon her marriage to my father.

I was a quiet child. Cousin Mary said I did not talk much because I was embarrassed by my birth defect. {Thanks, Cousin Mary.} I did not speak much because I did not have much to say. Cousin Mary expanded on her slander by saying that due to my "deformity" I could not suckle properly and therefore had to take all sustenance through a shot glass.

[Pours some whiskey into the shot glass and picks it up.]

Deformity or not, that part is true.

[Drinks then puts the shot glass down. He pours some whiskey into the larger glass as he continues to speak.]

But as I grew older, a shot glass was no longer large enough.

[He drinks.]

In 1863 my father moved us south, almost as far south as we could go and still remain in Georgia, for the duration of the war. My father bought approximately three thousand acres of land for just over $34,000.00. Such a high price. I don't think land will ever get more expensive than that. After the war, when Reconstruction came, the value of my father's land dropped to $1,700.00.

My mother kept me close to her most of the time because I was her only child. My older sister Martha died before I was born. She was only six months old.

Mother taught me at home for some time. Afterwards, I also attended the Valdosta Institute. Between my mother and my attendance at the Institute, I was schooled in languages, manners, mathematics, music, rhetoric, history, and many other subjects. In late 1864 my cousin Mattie came to live with us.

[Pulls a small framed photo out of his breast pocket.]

She was not quite two years my senior.

[Puts photo back in same pocket.]

She was also beautiful and charming and a breath of fresh air. When I was with Mattie there was a sense of peace I needed, that we all needed, after so many years of war. Mattie and I became very close.

One day I got into a disagreement with a chap at school and he challenged me to a duel. We were both all of fifteen years old at the time. When we gathered, my opponent's second had a set of pistols loaded with powder and paper but no bullets. "No thank you."

[Produces a pistol of his own.]

"I have brought my own, loaded and ready to go.

[Turns his back to his opponent, in profile to the audience. Turns head slightly to talk over his shoulder.]

What's that you say?...A mock duel? Certainly not! My pistol is fully loaded.

[He turns to fire.]

Where are you going?"

[He looks directly at the audience.]

"Back down" was never in my vocabulary.

[Puts pistol away.]

I saw the men of our town signing up, lining up and marching away. A sea of gray uniforms that grew larger and larger with each passing day. My father, like every other able-bodied man in Valdosta, volunteered to serve in the Confederate

Army. But his length of service was cut short. He was not killed in the war. Unlike most families in Valdosta, every member of the Holliday family who went to war came home. My father was not discharged from his position in the army because of some heinous act or even some heroic act he performed. He was released from service because he had chronic diarrhea. You might say the war gave him the shits.

We lived in Valdosta until the North's tragic victory. Many of the freedmen, the ex-slaves, thought that not only were they no longer slaves they also thought they were free from having to work at all. Many were kind to their former owners. Many were not. That goes both ways. Richard Force, a returning veteran of the war, was arrested for choking a negro. He escaped from jail but made the mistake of returning to his family home where, after a confrontation with soldiers, he was shot. He died five months later of blood poisoning.

Most of my family, myself included, hated the Northern Occupation. The only exception was my father. He worked for the Freedmen Bureau. (Incredulous) He was employed by the Northern Occupational Forces. Because of that, he lost all of the respect the community once had for him.

In September 16, 1866 my mother died. A day expected for a long time, for she had been ill and bedridden with consumption for over two years, but still a day that came far too soon for a fifteen-year-old boy. As I mentioned, my mother joined the

Presbyterian Church when she married my father; but she never accepted the doctrine of predestination. On her deathbed she very vocally rejected the Presbyterian Church and declared herself a Methodist.

During the funeral the Methodist minister praised my mother and her life, took a few swipes at the Presbyterian Church, and my mother was laid to rest.

The accepted practice was a year of mourning. The men wore black for nine months and grey for another three. Anything less would be considered an unforgivable slight to the departed. Yet only three months after my mother's death my father married Rachel Martin, our neighbor's twenty-three-year-old daughter. She was only eight years older than me, and she was ugly.

I promptly joined the Methodist Church.

[Takes another drink and lights a cigar. He thinks for a moment then draws his pistol.]

I became a dentist because of my education in the use of firearms.

[Sees confused looks on members of the audience.]

While my mother had schooled me in the arts, my father taught me about riding, hunting and the proper use of guns. Drawing fast was not as important as aiming straight.

There was a swimming hole my friends and I enjoyed. We went there one day and some negroes were throwing dirt and debris into the water, making it totally unusable. They refused to leave. That is fact. What happened next is where the stories multiply and divide. Some stories say I shot one negro dead and the rest ran off. The next story says I shot three dead. Bat Masterson, that bastard, said that I was responsible for the "indiscriminate" killing of some negroes.

No one died. That alone is proof I did not shoot at anyone. I never killed anyone who did not deserve it and this was not a capital offense. So, I fired over their heads and they ran off. However, tensions were still bad it being so soon after the war. So, I was sent for an extended visit to the home of my uncle Thomas McKey. My uncle encouraged me to seek further education, so I enrolled in the Pennsylvania College of Dental Surgery in Philadelphia. The course of study was two years, six days a week. Total cost: $105.00.

During those two years I operated on forty or so patients, filled some teeth, pulled others. As part of my training, between terms I returned to Valdosta and studied under a local dentist, Dr. Lucien Frank. My goal was to establish myself and then open a practice with my cousin Robert who was a year or so behind me in school.

As I said before, my schooling was six days a week. On the seventh day, I did not rest. My father thought I was attending church, but I was attending to my "worldly education". Philadelphia had many things to offer.

[Sound effect of party going on. He drinks and smokes, bows to unseen ladies.]

My mother did teach me how to dance and the proper way to court the ladies. I put those lessons to good use.

I graduated from dental school in good standing and returned to Valdosta. I joined a practice and started to make a good name for myself as a dentist. I performed some pretty extensive dental work on one patient. Sum of the bill: twenty-one dollars. Fees have not gone up since then, have they?

[There is a light change as he crosses the stage to indicate a passage in time.]

There has been much speculation as to why I left Georgia in such a rush, especially when my dental practice was so promising. Were my cousin Mattie and I closer than cousins ought to have been? Actually, cousins marrying was an accepted practice. However, it was not accepted by the Catholic Church and Mattie was a devout Catholic.

My dental practice was going well until I developed this little cough that would not go away. Patients did not like having my hands in their mouth in the first place. My constantly coughing in their faces was a definite client loser. I was diagnosed with consumption. My doctor told me I needed to live in a warmer, dryer climate and consume a moderate amount of wine.

"Moderate"?

And for this radical change in lifestyle I was told I might live another year. Another year. (I'd rather die tomorrow.)

It was decided I should head to the healthier climate of Dallas, Texas. Made no sense. Dallas and Georgia had similar climates. It was like moving across the continent in order to live in the house across the street. But westward I did go. I boarded the Western and Atlantic, bound for Dallas. My family was there, except for my father's young wife. I did not think of this until much later. I had done my best to not notice Rachel as much as possible. I would not have seen her at the station even if she was standing right next to me.

[Transition in lighting. He crosses the stage.]

I was on my own, but I did not travel alone. (Somber) Many ghosts came with me. Mistakes made, dreams unfulfilled, a love lost.

[Touches pocket where he placed the picture.]

I seem to remember having traveled through a great many towns in my life. Some were wonderful, full of life, full of excitement and possibilities. Some places I care not to remember, and I am sure the feeling is mutual.

I arrived in Dallas in 1872. Dallas.

[Takes a deep breath and smiles.]

Ahh, what a shit hole. The streets were not paved with cobblestones. Those were cow pies as far as you could see. The way the city cleaned up that mess was to allow hogs to roam the streets. But that created a problem of its own. In the year after my arrival, Dallas grew from a mud hole of a few hundred to a town of over seven thousand. One street alone had over forty saloons, gambling houses, and enough whores to fill them all. (Smiles) You'd think nothing could ever be better than that.

[Crosses to table as he continues to speak.]

However, I did find a doctor who insisted that the proper method of treatment for my consumption was to dramatically, drastically and immediately increase my intake of whiskey.

[Pours himself a large glass of whiskey and downs it.]

He was a brilliant man! I was not going to be alone in Dallas. I was to partner with an established dentist, John A. Seegar. That partnership did not last, though. On May 12, 1874 I was arrested for gambling. My times at the faro tables and poker tables did not set well with Dr. Seegar and his Baptist beliefs. Then again, neither did my carrying a gun or drinking whiskey on a daily basis. But the timing of our partnership dissolving was providential. About a month after I paid a fine of ten dollars for the gambling charge and left Dallas, the building that housed the dental practice burned to the ground.

My next town was Denison, about seventy-five miles from Dallas: bawdy houses, gambling dens. I felt right at home. But my time in Denison was not long either. I had made a little trip to Dallas to celebrate the New Year-1875. I had tired of all the firecrackers and so had this gent named Charlie Austin. We decided the night should be louder by shooting our guns...at each other. I was found not guilty of attempted murder and I left town, pretty much bypassing Denison and going on to Denver. On the road to Denver, I got off the stage in Ft. Griffin to stretch my legs when my eyes caught glimpse of the Beehive Saloon. Innocent curiosity got the better of me and I wandered over there. Met a big wind of a man named Hurricane Bill Martin. He was a regular at the poker and faro tables. One of his friends was a fellow named Curly Bill Brocious. Several weeks of stretching my legs later, I tired of Ft. Griffin and I finally arrived in Denver. Denver held so much interest for me that I left at the first available opportunity and headed for Cheyenne. From Cheyenne on to Deadwood. Yet even more gamblers and loose women.

One winter in Deadwood was more than enough. My lungs did not appreciate the cold and neither did the rest of me. So, once again I closed up shop and got a ticket for the stagecoach. I was making a straight line to Denver via a return trip to Ft. Griffin. First time I was there in two years. They had a new sheriff, John M. Larn. A charming gentleman who had the qualifications a growing community like Ft. Griffin needed in a sheriff: previous experience-as a cow thief and a killer. Between Sheriff Larn and the town vigilance committee I kept a low profile. I just spent my time at the gaming tables in order to earn enough to keep on going to wherever.

I left Ft. Griffin for a second, and hopefully last, time, and made my way to St. Louis. There I met a lady named Kate Fisher, also known as Kate Elder, Kate Harony, and Big Nosed Kate. If you ever saw a photograph of her you would understand how she got that name. She looked like an unmade bed, but her Hungarian accent intrigued me. She had left home at an early age and earned her way across the country in a manner she could not have learned from her strict Catholic upbringing. She was a woman of fine character. There has been much speculation as to the nature of our relationship. I always treated her with the utmost courtesy, and she was always totally professional with me. And when I left St. Louis, she came with me. We found ourselves in many towns and I sat on both sides of the gaming tables in most of them. Back in Griffin, I was dealing faro one night when a tall fellah with striking blue eyes came to my table: "What's your name, stranger?...Wyatt Earrp? Well, Mr. Earrp, lay your money down...You're a winner, Mr. Earr--all right, Wyatt."

[Pulls out knife while talking about Ed Bailey]

Not long afterwards, I was playing poker with Ed Bailey. One thing you do not do while playing poker is fiddle with the deadwood. Once a card is discarded it is not to be touched until the shuffle for the next hand.

"Leave the deadwood alone, Ed...Because I said so."

Ed was too stubborn and too foolish to follow my advice and kept touching the discards. So, as was my right, I claimed the pot without showing my cards. Ed started to skin his pistol when I drew a line on him from his belly to his heart.

[Uses knife to draw the line.]

Ed was a popular man in Griffin, so the law got involved. Sheriff Larn made me stay in my hotel room, with a deputy outside the door, while he sorted the whole mess out. The vigilance committee wanted to invite me to be guest of honor at a necktie party. Kate decided the best thing to do under the circumstances was to set fire to a shed. While the townspeople were pouring water on the fire, Kate and a pistol talked the deputy outside my door into allowing us to leave town.

Our next stop was Dodge City where the cattle trails ended at the poker tables and the saloons. Wyatt Earp was there too. Got himself a job as a deputy town marshal. The Long Branch was one of the finest saloons in town. There were a couple of dozen places. Some nice like the Long Branch. Some were not much more than a tent, a few tables, some kerosene lamps and a whiskey barrel. Outside of town there were cattle as far as you could see. You did not see grass. You saw longhorns packed so close together you could walk on their backs all the way to Texas without ever touching the ground. Or so it seemed. The men came in from the trails. Their pockets were full of cash and I wanted to do everything I could to help change that. But despite all of the people and the noise and excitement, Dodge was a dull town. Every night, things ended about two o'clock in the morning. Why the hell it ended so early I do not know.

On the night of September 24th, a man was about to shoot Wyatt in the back. What happened?...I saw him first.

[Smiles, then coughs]

Dodge's climate was not conducive to helping my consumption. So, once again Kate and I packed and headed to Las Vegas, New Mexico. "Las Vegas". Now that's a silly name for a gambling town. Don't think it will catch on.

But I did not go there just for the gambling. Las Vegas was close to the curative hot springs in nearby Gallinas Canyon. Many consumptives went there. (I always hated the term "lunger".) My health improved enough that I opened a dental office there. In the same building was a fellow consumptive, one William Leonard. Bill was a jeweler. We both worked with gold, but to different ends. Bill was an excellent jeweler and an even better shootist. Jose Mares learned the hard way of Bill's prowess with a gun. Instead of facing the murder indictment, Bill left town.

I left Las Vegas when gambling had been declared illegal. I was fined $25 dollars. I left town, having neglected to pay the fine or to bring Kate with me, and headed back to Dodge City. Kate did not join me because her business was still thriving.

I headed back to Dodge because I knew Wyatt was there. I liked him. Kate did not. She used to "work" for Wyatt's brother Jim and Jim's wife. She never much cared for any of the Earps.

Kate did eventually find her way to Dodge City. But she no sooner arrived than I left for Prescott, Arizona. Prescott was on the way to Tombstone where Wyatt was headed, and he said I should go there too. I had already paid for my passage and Kate earned the money for her ticket in short order.

No Nose Gordon got drunk the week before I arrived in Prescott and he was still drunk after I got there. He was called No Nose because it had been bitten off in a fight. Despite this un-natural deformity, he did have a regular lady friend. One night, he was trying to make this woman leave one saloon and go with him to another. She refused to go. He got mad and yelled out that he was going to get a gun and "either kill someone or be killed by someone." I happened to run into him on the street and...

[Lights a cigar and looks at someone in the audience]

You want to know what happened?

[Looks at someone else in the audience]

You explain it to him.

While in Prescott, I was playing poker one night with a young man by the name of William Bonney and a southern gentleman by the name of Jesse James. Mr. James had plenty of money to gamble with, having just robbed "one or two" northern trains. By doing so he had immediately earned my respect and for the first time in recent memory I did not cheat at cards that night. Not even once.

Wyatt sent me a letter urging me to continue on to Tombstone. His brother Virgil was a marshal there and Wyatt had become one too. The arrival of that one simple little letter caused one hell of a dust storm. Kate did not want to go to Tombstone. She gave me her reasons as I was packing.

"Yes, Kate, damn you. I am going to Tombstone...Because Wyatt asked me to...I don't care if you don't like him. I do...No, I don't think I will be there long. Not much going on in Tombstone, despite what Wyatt said. From what I have heard, it is a quiet town and not likely to change."

Kate did not want to be left behind, but she did not want to go all the way with me. {Keep your minds out of the gutter.} I left and she followed, but only as far as Gillette. She went on to Globe and I headed for Tombstone. I rode the stagecoach with a man named John Behan. He did not impress me much. Doubted I would ever see him again.

[He wanders the streets of Tombstone. Sound effect: Busy street, people going about their business, traffic.]

Tombstone was a solid community with a future, and a wide variety of businesses: Hotel, whorehouse, general store, saloon, picture gallery, saloon, saloon, whorehouse, gun store, saloon, hotel, saloon, saloon. There were many elegant saloons like the Oriental and the Alhambra. At the Oriental Milt Joyce ran the bar and the restaurant. The gaming room was run by Lou Richabaugh. I found work as a faro dealer at the Alhambra. John E. Tyler worked at the Danner and Owens Saloon as a dealer and troublemaker. When he was not dealing cards, he was to make trouble for the other saloons, try to drive business away. He tried to start a fight at Vogan and

Flynn's, but all parties were disarmed before anyone got shot. On October 10, 1880 I had a problem with Mr. Tyler myself. I do not recall if he tried to pick a fight with me or if I just took umbrage to his showing his ugly face in public. I had no sooner said, "John E. Tyler, hide your face! You're scaring the horses!" when he drew his gun. Of course mine was out as well; but the local sheriffs stepped in between us and confiscated our pistols. The guns were deposited at the bar at the Oriental, and we were told to go about our business. I went to the Oriental to retrieve my gun, but Milt Joyce refused to hand it over.

He said I was drunk and he was not about to give a firearm to a drunk. He emphasized his point by throwing me out, literally.

[Dusts himself off.]

I obtained another gun and went back to the Oriental. Milt charged at me. I charged at him. We tussled. We cussed and before we got pulled apart shots were fired. I was bleeding from the head. Someone had buffaloed me. Milt was shot in the hand. He hated my guts ever since then, and I thought even less of him.

I was arrested on a charge of attempted murder. But despite the fact that the Oriental was crowded that night, no witnesses against me appeared in court. Three were called: John Behan, West Fuller and Milt Joyce himself. They all failed to appear. I pleaded guilty to a charge of assault and battery and paid a fine of $25.00 plus $11.25 in court costs.

In December of 1880 Curly Bill Brocious, after having had several drinks, decided it was his duty to shoot out all of the street lamps. Wyatt grabbed him from behind, pinning his arms, as Marshal Fred White tried to disarm him.

"You goddamnsonofabitch, let go of that pistol!" Fred certainly had a way with words.

As Fred was taking Curly's gun away it went off, sending a bullet into Fred just below the belt and up into his chest. Fred lingered for several days before he died. He was much loved in Tombstone and Curly Bill was taken to Tucson to avoid a lynching. Before he died, Fred gave a deathbed declaration that the shooting had been an accident. So Curly Bill was set free.

The first part of 1881 saw so many shootings in the Oriental that Milt Joyce closed the gaming room. That ended my desire to go there and even John E. Tyler stayed away. John Behan became a county sheriff, which made one more reason for me to not like him. Behan looked the other way when Ike Clanton and his family and the McLaurys and the other the Cowboys wanted him to, which was most of the time. They had a thriving cattle business. They went across the border to Mexico, stole cattle and brought it back up here to sell.

Ike Clanton's father was shot and killed by some Mexicans who took umbrage at being robbed. Behan had taken up with a woman, an actress named Josephine Marcus. He was at my faro table one night, making more of an ass out of himself than usual.

That was something Behan often did with very little effort. I had had enough of his mouth so I told him the game was over as far as he was concerned.

"Go on, Johnny. You're only playing with money I gave to your woman earlier."

My comment made Josephine look bad and embarrassed Behan in front of his friends. It also did not help that Wyatt had caught Josephine's eye recently and they were spending a good deal of time together.

Kate came for a visit and she tried again to get me to move back to Globe with her. She was running a hotel. Had hourly rates...So did the hotel. But I was not interested and I told her so.

My friend Bill Leonard had moved to Tombstone in 1880. Time and consumption had treated him harshly. Unfortunately, he made friends with the wrong people. Instead of making jewelry, he took items his new friends had stolen and melted them down for the gold. On March 15th, 1881 the Kinnear and Company stagecoach was robbed and the driver, Bud Philpot, was killed. One of the robbers was identified as Bill Leonard and because people in Tombstone knew he and I were friends-I never tried to hide it-it was assumed I also had to have been involved. Well, I was not involved. If I wanted someone's money there is always poker. The day of the robbery I had rented a horse for an afternoon's ride. On my way back I came across Old Man Fuller who was bringing his water wagon to Tombstone. I hitched my horse to his wagon and rode into town with him. Wyatt's brother Warren came to my room and told me Wyatt needed to see me, friend to friend and not in his capacity as a deputy marshal. He told me what Bill had done. The damned fool! Guilt by association. It was all rumors. I was fighting the rumors and I was fighting with Kate. Once I told her what Wyatt had told me, she pushed even harder for me to leave Tombstone with her.

"I can't leave now, Kate...Because it would make even more people think I was guilty. Now get the hell out!"

Kate stormed out of our room and ran right into Behan and Milt Joyce. Sheriff Behan, still stinging from our confrontation at the faro table, wanted to do what he could to put me in jail for the robbery and for Philpot's murder. Also, Milt's hand had healed but he was still smarting.

Let me give you all a couple of pieces of advice. One: try not to shoot anybody if you can possibly avoid it. Two: If you have to shoot someone, don't just wound him in the hand or he may go on to become a county supervisor with enough clout to get you indicted.

Behan came to me on July 5th and arrested me for the robbery and for the murder of Bud Philpot.

"You're arresting me? On what evidence?"

[He is handed an affidavit. He reads it out loud.]

"John Henry Holliday, also known as Doc Holliday, did confess to me that he had taken part in the robbery that resulted in the death of Bud Philpot..."

[Reads part of it silently.]

"Signed by Kate Fisher!"

"Kate, why the hell would you do such a thing? What would possess you to be so stupid?...You got drunk and Behan made you sign the affidavit?...Get out of my sight!!"

Drunk? Kate could drink the entire Texas Rangers under the table. Well, later that day she certainly tried because Virgil Earp arrested Kate for being drunk in public. She paid a fine of twelve dollars and fifty cents. She could always break a ten.

In the four days between my arrest and my court date, Kate changed her story three or four times. I went from having killed Bud Philpot myself to just being "heavily involved" to being only partially involved to having nothing to do with the robbery at all. Justice Spicer, seeing that the only evidence against me was Kate and her word, dismissed the charges. But the damage had been done. The accusation was enough.

In late October, Virgil asked me if I wanted to join in on a poker game with him and a few others. I told him I was going to head back to the hotel and get a good night's sleep. Seems like a quiet evening. I think it will be a quiet day tomorrow as well.

[Quick blackout followed immediately by gunfire. The gunfire, and accompanying flashes on stage, lasts for thirty seconds. This will allow the actor playing the time needed to put on his long coat. He stands slightly downstage of center. After the gunfire ceases, there is a moment of silence and then a flood light comes up on Doc. He is holding his pistol.]

Guess I was wrong about it being quiet around here.

[Puts gun down or away.]

Perhaps I should tell you the events that led up to the shooting which, by the way, did not happen in the O.K. Corral but down the street from the corral. But "the shooting down the street" does not have much of a ring to it. I was sound asleep. It was the middle of the night when Kate burst into the room and woke me up.

"Kate, now why the hell are you waking me up at the ungodly hour of twelve noon? You know my day does not start until two...Oh, Ike Clanton is looking for me? Well, if God lets me live long enough to get my clothes on, he shall see me..."

I was awake and dressed and decided to do what was necessary-have breakfast. On my way a nice young man named Billy Clanton rode into town. I greeted him, shook his hand and went about my business. After breakfast, I decided to head over to the Alhambra when Morgan met me and told me all that had been happening since the night before. There had been that poker game with Virgil, Tom Mclaury, John Behan and Ike Clanton. Ike was Billy Clanton's older brother. Ike lost, as he usually did, and he got upset as he usually did. He drank more. The more he drank, the more upset he got and the more he lost. He said he had been cheated. Well, Ike was doing the cheating and he was bad enough at it to get caught. He was told to go home and sober up. Virgil went home to bed. The rest of the party went home and to sleep. Ike, however, stayed up the rest of the night, drinking, cussing and swearing he would get the Earps. Went to every saloon that was open, which was all of them. Kept saying he had been insulted by the Earps. Well, if calling a man a cheater at cards is insulting him, I guess he was being insulted. Somewhere along the way he decided he was going to get me too. Again, guilt by association. Kate got wind of this and that is when she woke me up in the middle of the night. Morgan too wanted to warn me that Ike had been shooting his mouth off. I wanted to shoot it off myself. But I didn't pay Ike any mind. I played cards with him often enough to know he was an idiot. He didn't even know how to cheat properly. But he was gonna "kill the Earps." There was "gonna be hell to pay." "The Earps and that Holliday feller are going to be dead."

He remembered the supposed insult. What he didn't remember was to bring a gun with him. He did try to buy a gun at Spangenberg's Gun Shop, but they wouldn't sell him one. So he went empty-handed to join the others at the corral. Ike was either drunk or stupid...or both. The Clantons and the McLaurys all claimed that they were not looking for trouble. If that were the case, why did they spend so much time in the gun store?

Billy Clanton said he was a man of peace. He said this as he was loading cartridges into his gun belt.

Virgil met Wyatt, Morgan and myself on the street and said to us:

"Some sons of bitches have been looking for a fight and now they can have it."

Virgil's plan was to leave them alone as long as they stayed in the O.K. Corral, but if they came out onto the street we would arrest them for carrying firearms within the city limits. I started to walk with Wyatt, Virgil and Morgan when Wyatt told me this was none of my affair.

"That is a hell of a thing for you to say to me...I know it's going to be a tough one. Tough ones are the kind I like."

I handed Virgil my cane and he handed me his shotgun. I think I got the better end of that deal. As we were approaching the corral, Johnny Behan told us that he had already disarmed everyone and we did not need to confront them. But he declined to come with us as we continued on our way.

Now I have been accused of firing the first shot. I cannot confirm this...Neither can I deny it. In any case, I may or may not have fired the first shot but, as is my habit, I most certainly did fire the last. It matters not who shot who, except when one of those sonsofbitches shot me across the back it did not help my otherwise sunny disposition. What mattered when that thirty seconds had passed is that most of the gang had scattered. Ike ran like shit through a pig before it all started. Frank and Tom McLaury and Billy Clanton were mortally wounded. Virgil was shot in the leg, Morgan was hit in both shoulders, I was creased across the back and Wyatt was shot in the coat...He loved that coat.

The McLaurys and Clanton were carried to a nearby store where Frank and Tom expired almost immediately. Billy Clanton lived long enough to tell people to get the hell away from him, but not before they gave him more cartridges for his gun. When it was all over, there was a deafening silence. I think our ears were still ringing from the shooting. When the smoke finally cleared, Behan emerged from his hiding place and tried to arrest us. Wyatt gave him a look right in the eyes and said, "I don't think so." I am not sure, but I think at that moment Behan soiled himself before he said he had other business to attend to and left.

But we were eventually arrested and charged with murder, due in part to the arrival of William McLaury from Texas. He was a lawyer and brother to Frank and Tom. During the trial I took detailed notes. I wanted to take the stand and refute everything that lying, no good sonofabitch Ike Clanton was saying about me. But for some reason our defense attorneys thought I was "too volatile" and they put Wyatt on the stand instead.

All of the Earp women stood by their men. Mattie Earp was less and less in the picture. Josie Marcus was more in the forefront. There was a fire there; but that is another story. Kate showed her loyalty to me by leaving town.

"You're leaving me, Kate?...Going back to Globe, are ya? How did you get the fare for the stagecoach? No, that is a silly question...You met a man at the hotel named John Ringo who gave it to you? How many times did you have to give it to him?"

That last moment we saw each other, before we parted for what would be the last time, I looked deep into her eyes. There was nothing there-all the way to the back of her head.

I never saw her again. She and I never married, as she would later claim time and again; and she did not come to my bedside in Glenwood Springs. Neither did I send her any letter imploring her to come. In fact, besides the young man who brought me my daily whiskey, my only two visitors were Father Downey-a Catholic priest and Reverend Rudolph-a Presbyterian minister. (I couldn't find a Methodist.) I invited them both to come talk to me because I wanted to hedge my bets. And by the way, there is no truth to the rumor that I drank two quarts of whiskey a day. Why stop at two?

But I digress.

No matter what Judge Spicer decided on the case, there would be some who would like it and there would be some who would not. Spicer concluded that the homicides happened during the execution of lawful duty. We were exonerated. Many cheered. William McLaury was not among them. He and Ike Clanton did everything they could to have the charges refiled and have myself and the Earps put in prison. Many people were so overjoyed at Spicer's ruling that they felt the need to write to the newspaper:

[Pulls newspaper clipping out of pocket.]

To Judge Wells Spicer-- Sir, if you take my advice you will take your departure for a more genial clime, as I don't think this one healthy for you much longer. It is only a matter of time. You will get it sooner or later.

[He puts the newspaper away.]

That about sums up the way most of the people made the Earps and me feel wanted. We all moved to the Cosmopolitan Hotel and always traveled in groups. Things quieted down for a while. We were actually beginning to feel like we were going to be allowed to stay, and live, in Tombstone.

[He crosses downstage right. The lights dim to suggest evening.]

On the night of December 28th, Virgil was heading for home from the Oriental when shotgun blasts, fired by cowards in the shadows, cut him down. His left arm was shattered and he would never be able to use it again. But he did tell his wife, "I've still got one arm to hug you with." He did tell Wyatt one thing that set in motion a chain of events that would carry us to many places. Virgil told Wyatt that as he was coming out of the Oriental, he did see Frank Stilwell go into the building where the shots had come from. Wyatt was appointed a Deputy United States Marshall. He deputized several men including myself.

In early January, Johnny Ringo challenged me to a handkerchief duel.

[He pulls a handkerchief out of his pocket.]

Each man holds onto one end of the handkerchief. That is all the distance between them, all the distance between Johnny Ringo and me.

"I'm your huckleberry. That's just my game."

But we were pulled apart by several witnesses.

A couple of months later, Morgan, Dan Tipton and I attended the theatre, a play called "Stolen Kisses". After the show, I went back to my rooms. Morgan went to play billiards at Campbell & Hatch's. "Good night, Morgan. I will see you tomorrow."

[There is the loud sound of a gunshot and glass shattering. The lights slightly dim on stage until a flood light covers Doc.]

The bullet entered Morgan's back and pretty much tore up everything inside. His spine was destroyed. He languished for forty minutes. Morgan told Wyatt, who had witnessed the shooting of his younger brother, "They got me, Wyatt. Don't let them get you."...and he died. Again the name of Frank Stilwell was mentioned as having been seen in the vicinity.

Wyatt changed that night. We came to an agreement on what had to be done. He and I did not speak a word, but much was said in the silence. The next day was Wyatt's 34th birthday.

[Lights come up to normal.]

Morgan was to be taken to the family home in Colton, California. His coffin was put on the train in Tucson. Someone said Frank Stilwell was seen near the station. Wyatt and I and a couple of others rode back to Tombstone after we saw the train off with Virgil, his wife and Morgan.

Several hours after the train left Tucson, and we were well on our way back to Tombstone, Frank Stilwell's body was found near the tracks. They could not tell how he died, but I would venture a guess that it was probably one or more of the thirty plus bullets that were found in his body. I do not know that I am in any way responsible for his death.

[Smiles ruefully]

But I did have to reload my guns that night...more than once.

On the day we got back to Tombstone, a telegram had been sent to Sheriff Behan to inform him that we were wanted for the murder of Frank Stilwell. Fortunately, the telegraph agent was a friend of Wyatt's and by the time Behan got the telegram, around eight that evening, we had come and gone.

Wyatt and I had done a lot of riding together and made many pay their debt. Among them, Curly Bill Brocious was "One more for Morg". But it was decided that we should part company for a while. There was no argument, no falling out as many unknowing tongues have claimed. At Trinidad, Colorado we said our goodbyes. Wyatt went his way and I went to Pueblo. I spent some time there before moving on to Denver.

On May 16 this little troll of a man, named Perry Mallon, shoved two pistols in my direction and announced that I was under arrest for: The murder of Frank Stilwell. The murder of Curly Bill Brocious (which Mallon claimed to have personally witnessed). The murder of Billy Clanton. The attempted murder of Ike Clanton (That alone was an insult, insinuating I had ever missed a target.) The murder of a conductor on the Southern Pacific railroad and the murder of Mallon's partner in Utah. I was in Denver at the time of that supposed shooting. Now while I am a good shot, even I would be hard pressed to shoot someone over three hundred miles away. Mallon's story changed every time he spoke to someone, and he made a point of talking to anyone who would listen. At first Mallon was a marshal from Los Angeles. Then he was a marshal from Arizona. It finally came out that he was no lawman. He had no partner in Utah. He did come here to arrest me but also to collect the $500 John Behan had offered him.

I knew that if I was sent back to Arizona, I would never stand trial. The cowboys would be waiting for me, with their guns drawn and ready. But I was never sent to Arizona. A few men did their utmost to make sure I never left the State of Colorado. One of these men was Bat Masterson. Oh, he did not come to my aid out of any affection for me. He didn't like me and said so on many occasions. I never cared much for him either. But I do give Bat credit for one thing: He was a loyal friend to Wyatt and he knew that not only did Wyatt like me but that I was just as fond of Wyatt. Bat was saving the friend of a friend. He made sure I was charged with a count of larceny in Pueblo. State charges would have to be dealt with before any talk of extradition would be considered. The wheels of justice ground particularly slow in Colorado.

[Smiles]

It was later proven that Perry Mallon was nothing more than a confidence man. His image, as well as his story, was printed in newspapers across the country. Seems a great many people in Ohio knew him. "Liar" and "thief" were the words they used most often to describe him. And a gentleman named Rublee remembered meeting Mallon in Omaha two years earlier. He also remembered

the amount of money Mallon had conned out of him. Rublee's account was published in the Denver Tribune. When Mallon demanded proof, the Tribune furnished it as Rublee was by then living in Denver. Mallon had to return three times the amount of money he had stolen from Rublee. When Mallon realized he was being found out and he was not going to get any rewards for my arrest, he borrowed money from several people and promptly disappeared. Among the many people looking for him were the wife and daughter he abandoned in Utah, as well as another wife in Ohio.

[Coughing gets worse]

Two days later, the body of John Ringo was found in Morse's Canyon east of Tombstone. A single gunshot wound to the head. Again, I wish I could take credit but I was in Leadville, Colorado at the time. Leadville had one hundred twenty saloons, one hundred eighteen gambling halls, one hundred ten beer gardens and thirty-five brothels. So I had three hundred eighty-three reasons to be there. But one major reason existed to send me away.

[Coughs]

Leadville was the last place consumptives should be. The climate was not at all hospitable and even literature on the town mentions this. I had kept in touch with only one member of my family after I left home, and that was my cousin Mattie. She was always devoutly religious, a strong Catholic. On October 1, 1883 she became Sister Mary Melanie of the Sisters of Mercy. So, God took the only woman I ever truly loved.

I left Leadville and found myself in many places. I passed through Galveston, staying only briefly. I was almost immediately followed by a yellow fever epidemic. I cannot say which visit caused the citizens of Galveston more alarm. My hands were no longer steady enough to hold cards. My coughing was to the point where no one would hire me as a faro dealer.

In Denver, I was walking through the lobby of the Windsor Hotel. Wyatt and Josephine had been meeting friends and I wanted to see him one last time. We talked of many things, the time I stopped him from getting shot in the back, Tombstone, and sometimes we did not talk at all. But, again, much was said in the silence.

[He stands to go and looks quietly at Wyatt. He is crying.]

"Good-bye, my old friend. It will be a long time before we meet again."

[He looks about the stage and finally speaks directly to the audience. The light starts to dim until a small spotlight directly overhead Doc is all the light that is left.]

And I must take my leave of you as well. I thank you for listening to this old ghost. Please do me a favor. When you leave here tonight, go to your own Long Branch or Oriental and have one for me...and know that you now have a ghost traveling with you.

[The spotlight goes out. Doc exits. A blue light comes up on the bed.]

THE END

CPSIA information can be obtained
at www.ICGtesting.com
Printed in the USA
LVHW011302041119
636244LV00012B/5325